While the author has taken great pains to deliver you a book filled with wisdom, they don't claim it's flawless. The book is provided 'as is', and any use of the information it contains is at your own risk.

The methods detailed in this book are the author's personal musings and should not be seen as the only way to reach the intended goal. There's always room for interpretation and personal growth.

Despite its wisdom, this book does not contain medical advice. The author may know a thing or two about life and the universe, but they're not a doctor. Always consult with a healthcare provider before embarking on new health journeys.

This book is meant to enlighten and entertain. If you manage to trip over a nugget of wisdom, great! But any repercussions are yours to bear, not the author's or publisher's.

If you don't agree with these terms, you're welcome to return your purchase.

Published by White Sands, LLC

ISBN: 979-8-9886503-3-1

Higher Wisdom

Insights from Ancient Masters to Modern Minds

Scribed and Sketched by Orion Myst

DEDICATION

To Wendy, the light of my life, whose love nurtures the seeds of my being, enabling me to blossom. Your strength and wisdom ground me, your love elevates me. Together we create a beautiful symphony.

To our sons, Skylar and Cameron, each of you is a brilliant star in our shared universe. Your laughter is the melody that fills our home with joy, your curiosity is the compass guiding our adventures. As you journey through life, may each step you take deepen your understanding, expand your compassion, and illuminate your unique path.

To Forrest, though our paths have diverged, you are always with me, carried in every heartbeat, reflected in every thought. In every word of this book, may you find a beacon that guides you back to our shared harbor.

I extend this dedication to our cherished family of friends - Mykael, Kipper, Aiden, Meko, Chris, and Rachel. The bonds we share transcend conventional definitions, for you are family not by blood, but by love. Our shared laughter, tears, conversations, and silences weave a vibrant tapestry of connection and mutual respect. May this book serve as a reflection of our shared journey towards consciousness and love.

Lastly, to all the seekers, wanderers, and pathfinders, this book is a testament to the unending quest for enlightenment. As you turn each page, may you find a spark of wisdom, a moment of peace, and a ray of love that guides you home to your true self.

May the combined wisdom contained herein inspire you, guide you, and most importantly, remind you of the immense capacity for love and understanding within your own heart.

PREFACE

In the vast expanse of human existence, we often find ourselves lost, searching for a beacon, a guiding light to illuminate the path of wisdom and insight. This book, dear reader, is my humble attempt to be that beacon.

Throughout the course of my life, I have been fortunate to encounter wisdom in the most unlikely places—both external and within the recesses of my soul. These encounters have shaped me, challenged me, and ultimately, guided me on an extraordinary journey of self-discovery and enlightenment. This book encapsulates the distillation of my experiences, learning, and the profound wisdom I have gleaned through years of introspection and exploration.

You may find some ideas presented here to be familiar, like old friends you've known for years, while others may seem new, even challenging. I urge you to approach them with an open heart and mind. After all, our journey towards enlightenment is personal and unique to each of us, a path shaped by our individual experiences, perspectives, and understandings.

This book is not a prescription, nor is it a quick fix to the trials and tribulations of life. Instead, it's an invitation—an invitation to join me on a journey towards greater wisdom, understanding, and insight. It's a call to awaken the latent wisdom within you, to look beyond the obvious, to question, to seek, and to discover the profound that lies beneath the ordinary.

To my wife Wendy, my sons Skylar and Cameron, and my cherished family of friends, thank you for your unwavering love and support. Your presence has been a source of strength and inspiration. To Forrest, though distant in presence, you are ever close in my heart. This book, in its essence, is dedicated to you all and to every individual on their path of enlightenment.

As you turn these pages, my sincere hope is that the wisdom and insights shared within will resonate with you, provoke thought, and inspire a journey of discovery that is as rewarding and enlightening as mine has been.

Walk with me, dear reader, as we embark together on this extraordinary journey of wisdom and insight.

TABLE OF CONTENTS

INTRODUCTION

Embarking on the Journey of Higher Wisdom

Every human being embarks on a personal journey to seek wisdom and understanding, a quest that spans across time and space, cultures and philosophies. Our paths intertwine with the wisdom of ancient masters, the insight of modern minds, the shared experiences of stoner culture, and the transcendental realizations from psychedelic explorations. As we traverse this intricate matrix of knowledge, we come to understand that wisdom is not exclusive or restrictive; it is instead an infinite tapestry woven from the threads of diverse philosophies and experiences.

Wisdom is like the water that nourishes the tree of life. Just as the tree pulls water from the deep earth, sprouting leaves that reach toward the sky, our pursuit of wisdom allows us to grow and stretch, grounding us and elevating us simultaneously. We draw nourishment from the deep wells of ancient wisdom imparted by Socrates, Buddha, Lao Tzu, and many others. These ancient masters, each in their unique ways, delved into the complexities of human existence, asking timeless questions and offering insights that still resonate with us.

Fast forward to the present day, where our world is remarkably different from the times of these ancient masters. However, the core human quest for understanding and fulfillment remains the same. Modern philosophers and thinkers continue the tradition of unraveling life's mysteries, their words echoing in academic halls and the bustling urban jungle, on screens of various sizes and in quiet, introspective spaces.

In this quest for higher wisdom, we encounter subcultures and pathways that may seem unconventional, yet are rich in insights and teachings. The stoner philosophy, a byproduct of counterculture movements, offers a distinctive perspective on life and existence. Despite stereotypes and misconceptions, this philosophy offers profound wisdom about mindfulness, acceptance, and the pursuit of peace.

Finally, we delve into the realm of the extraordinary—psychedelic wisdom. Here, the mind expands beyond the ordinary, perceiving reality through a prism that refracts into multiple dimensions of understanding. Those who venture into this realm often return with intriguing insights and fresh perspectives that can illuminate our everyday existence.

As we journey through this book, remember that wisdom does not come from a single source or a singular experience. It is a synthesis of various teachings, experiences, and insights. Our exploration covers the breadth of human understanding from antiquity to modernity, from the earthly to the ethereal. And at the core of this exploration is you—the reader, the seeker. May you find in these pages the seeds of wisdom that resonate with you, inspire you, and guide you in your journey towards a more enlightened and fulfilled existence. Embark on this journey, not as a passive passenger but as an active explorer, for every step you take in the pursuit of higher wisdom brings you closer to understanding the greatest mystery of all—yourself.

Exercise: Sacred Space Creation

Creating a sacred space in your home can serve as a physical embodiment of your inner spiritual life, an outward expression of your internal journey. A sacred space is not merely an area designated for peace and quiet; rather, it is an environment where you can meditate, self-reflect, express gratitude, or partake in any activity that enriches your spiritual well-being. Here's a simple guide to creating a sacred space:

1. **Choose Your Spot**: The first step is to find a suitable place in your home. It could be a quiet corner in your bedroom, a portion of your living room, or even a spot in your backyard. The place should be somewhere you feel comfortable, at ease, and, most importantly, undisturbed.

2. **Cleanse the Area**: Clean your chosen area physically. You may also want to cleanse it spiritually with methods like smudging, using sound (like a bell or a singing bowl), or visualizing a light that purifies the space.

3. **Make it Comfortable**: Add elements

like a soft rug, a comfortable chair, or a cushion to sit on. The aim is to make this space inviting, a place where you want to spend time.

4. **Add Personal Touches**: Decorate your sacred space with objects that have spiritual significance to you. It can be anything: a photograph, a cherished memento, crystals, incense, candles, a statue of a deity, or spiritual symbols.

5. **Nature Connection**: If possible, incorporate elements of nature into your sacred space. It could be a potted plant, a bowl of sea shells, a vase of flowers, or even a window view to a garden.

6. **Create an Altar**: An altar is a focal point of a sacred space. It's a surface where you can arrange items that are spiritually meaningful to you. The act of

setting up an altar is a meditation in itself.

Chapter Summary

- Wisdom is an infinite tapestry woven from diverse philosophies and experiences; it is not exclusive or restrictive.
- Wisdom, much like water, nourishes the tree of life, allowing us to grow both in depth (grounding) and in height (elevation).
- The quest for understanding and fulfillment is an enduring human pursuit, dating back to ancient philosophers like Socrates, Buddha, and Lao Tzu, and continuing with modern thinkers.
- Unconventional pathways, such as the stoner philosophy and psychedelic experiences, offer distinctive perspectives and rich insights about life and existence.

- Psychedelic wisdom allows the mind to expand beyond ordinary perceptions and gain fresh perspectives that can illuminate everyday existence.
- Wisdom is not derived from a single source or experience, but a synthesis of various teachings, experiences, and insights.
- The core of this exploration is the reader, who is encouraged to actively engage in this journey of seeking wisdom.
- The pursuit of higher wisdom brings one closer to understanding the greatest mystery – oneself.

CHAPTER 1

The Ancient Masters

Our quest for wisdom begins in the dusty corridors of antiquity, where great thinkers first posed the questions that continue to define our human experience. These ancient masters—Socrates, Buddha, Lao Tzu, and others—embarked on intellectual journeys that laid the foundation for philosophical thought and spiritual wisdom.

Socrates, the father of Western philosophy, challenged the status quo of Athenian society, urging his fellow citizens to turn their gaze inward. His guiding principle, "Know thyself," serves as a beacon in our quest for understanding. For Socrates, wisdom begins with an acknowledgment of our own ignorance. This humble admission makes way for curiosity, inquiry, and, ultimately, a deeper understanding of oneself and the world.

Moving eastwards, we meet Buddha, whose teachings continue to illuminate the path towards inner peace and contentment. Buddha enlightened humanity with the Four Noble Truths, elucidating the existence of suffering, its origins, its cessation, and the path leading to the end of suffering. His guidance towards mindfulness, compassion, and detachment provides a timeless antidote to the stresses of our contemporary lives.

In ancient China, Lao Tzu penned the Tao Te Ching, a foundational text of Taoism. His wisdom emphasizes harmony with the Tao—the natural, spontaneous, and ever-changing flow of the universe.

He urged us to act effortlessly, in accordance with nature, teaching that "In the pursuit of knowledge, every day something is added. In the practice of the Tao, every day something is dropped."

Each of these masters offered unique pearls of wisdom, yet a common thread weaves through their teachings—a call for introspection, awareness, and harmony with the self and the world. Their wisdom, although thousands of years old, resonates in the modern era as we grapple with similar existential questions.

The philosophy of Socrates encourages us to challenge our assumptions, inspiring a lifelong quest for knowledge. Buddha's teachings guide us towards a peaceful and compassionate existence, fostering resilience in the face of life's inevitable challenges. Lao Tzu's wisdom reminds us to move with the currents of life rather than against them, advocating for a life of simplicity and contentment.

In essence, the wisdom of these ancient masters invites us to journey inward, to explore the vast landscapes of our minds, and to seek harmony with the world. Their teachings are not relics of a bygone era but rather timeless guideposts illuminating our path towards wisdom and understanding. As we move through this chaotic, ever-changing world, let's carry their insights with us, like a lantern that lights the way in the darkest of nights.

Exercise: The Practice of Mindful Eating

Eating mindfully elevates our mealtime from a mere task on our checklist to an exercise in awareness and appreciation. It engages all our senses, deepens our connection with food, and bolsters our overall well-being.

ACTION PLAN

1. **Prepare for Mindful Eating**: Eliminate distractions such as the television, smartphone, or laptop. Make sure you

are comfortably seated with your food in front of you, prepared to devote your full attention to the experience of eating.

2. **Engage All Senses**: Before diving in, take a moment to observe your food. Notice the colors and textures, and take in its aroma. Consider its journey to your plate—from the earth it was nurtured in to the hands that lovingly prepared it. This step cultivates a sense of appreciation and readies you for mindful consumption.

3. **Savor Each Bite**: Consume your food in small portions and chew each mouthful thoroughly. This aids digestion and allows you to fully experience all the flavors. Aim to chew each mouthful around 30 times.

4. **Recognize Your Body's Signals**: Tune

in to your body's cues. Begin eating when you experience genuine physical hunger. As you consume your food, stay aware of your body's indications of satiety, and cease eating before you feel uncomfortably full.

5. **Express Gratitude**: Upon concluding your meal, take a moment to express your appreciation. This could be a simple thank you for the nourishment your body has received, recognition of the individuals involved in preparing your meal, or gratitude for the Earth that produced the ingredients.

6. **Practice Consistently**: Like all new skills, mindful eating requires consistent practice. Begin with one meal each day and gradually extend this practice to all meals. Remember, the goal is not perfection, but rather the journey

towards greater presence and intentionality in your eating habits.

The adoption of mindful eating into our daily routines encourages a healthier relationship with food and enhances our overall enjoyment of life. Each meal becomes an opportunity to embrace mindfulness, transforming an everyday act into a moment filled with joy, awareness, and gratitude.

Chapter Summary

- The ancient masters, including Socrates, Buddha, and Lao Tzu, laid the foundation for philosophical thought and spiritual wisdom.
- Socrates, known as the father of Western philosophy, advocated for self-knowledge and acknowledged that wisdom begins with realizing our own ignorance.

- Buddha's teachings center on the Four Noble Truths, which discuss the existence, origin, cessation of suffering, and the path leading to its end. His teachings encourage mindfulness, compassion, and detachment.
- Lao Tzu, the author of the Tao Te Ching, emphasized harmony with the Tao, the natural and ever-changing flow of the universe. His teachings inspire us to act in accordance with nature and promote simplicity and contentment.
- The teachings of these ancient masters share a common theme: introspection, awareness, and harmony with the self and the world.
- Socratic philosophy encourages questioning assumptions and promotes a lifelong pursuit of knowledge.
- Buddha's wisdom guides us toward peace and resilience, while Lao Tzu's teachings remind us to move with life's currents rather than against them.
- The wisdom of these ancient masters remains relevant today, providing timeless guideposts on our path towards wisdom and

understanding. They encourage an inward journey and seeking harmony with the world.

CHAPTER 2

Modern Minds

As we emerge from the ancient corridors of wisdom, we step into the realm of modernity. The echoes of ancient philosophies resonate through the ages, reaching the ears of modern thinkers who add their unique voices to the symphony of wisdom. These modern minds have sifted through the sands of time, extracting relevant insights and overlaying them with contemporary perspectives.

Let's take a moment to consider the existentialists, for example. Jean-Paul Sartre and Albert Camus explored the essence of individual existence and freedom. They wrestled with questions of meaning, choice, and authenticity. Sartre, with his famous phrase "Existence precedes essence," highlights the freedom and responsibility each individual has to create their own life's meaning.

In the realm of psychology, thinkers like Carl Jung and Abraham Maslow expanded our understanding of the human mind. Jung explored the collective unconscious, shared symbols, and archetypes, broadening our perspective on human behavior and spiritual experiences. Maslow, with his hierarchy of needs, underlined the importance of self-actualization, positioning it as the pinnacle of human motivation.

In the world of contemporary philosophy and spirituality, figures like Eckhart Tolle and Thich Nhat Hanh guide us towards mindfulness and presence. Tolle's concept of "The Power of Now" emphasizes the importance of being present and conscious in the current moment, a profound call to action in our fast-paced, future-oriented world. Thich Nhat Hanh, Zen master and peace activist, teaches the art of mindful living, making every action a pathway to peace and joy.

The wisdom of these modern minds enhances our understanding of the world and ourselves. Sartre and Camus remind us of our individual freedom and the responsibility we bear in crafting our own lives. The psychological insights of Jung and Maslow help us navigate our inner worlds and motivations. The teachings of Tolle and Thich Nhat Hanh guide us towards mindful living, urging us to root ourselves firmly in the present moment.

The insights of these modern thinkers, when combined with the wisdom of ancient masters, create a comprehensive tapestry of knowledge. This tapestry, rich with diverse threads of wisdom, is a tool to aid us on our path towards understanding, self-fulfillment, and inner peace. As we navigate the journey of life, let us carry these insights in our minds and hearts, allowing them to inform, guide, and inspire us.

Exercise: Mindfulness Meditation Practice

Mindfulness meditation is a practice that involves paying focused attention to the present moment, accepting it without judgment. It helps cultivate a sense of peace, reduces stress, and improves overall well-being. Let's dive into a simple yet effective mindfulness meditation practice that you can incorporate into your daily life.

1. **Find a Quiet Space**: Choose a calm and quiet space where you can meditate without interruptions. It could be a peaceful corner of your home, a serene spot in your garden, or any place where you feel comfortable and at ease.

2. **Set a Timer**: Decide on the length of your meditation. If you're new to meditation, start with a shorter duration like 5 or 10 minutes. Gradually increase the time as your concentration improves.

3. **Assume a Comfortable Position**: Sit comfortably on a cushion, chair, or meditation mat. Ensure your back is straight but relaxed. You can also meditate while lying down if it is more comfortable for you.

4. **Close Your Eyes and Take Deep Breaths**: Gently close your eyes and take a few deep breaths. Feel the sensation of the breath entering and leaving your nostrils. This helps to relax your body and brings your focus to the present moment.

5. **Observe Your Breath**: Now, let your breath return to its natural rhythm. Pay attention to the sensation of your breath as it moves in and out. If your mind starts to wander, gently bring it back to your breath.

6. **Accept Your Thoughts**: During your meditation, you might notice thoughts, feelings, or sensations arising. Don't try to push them away. Instead, acknowledge them without judgment and then return your attention to your breath.

7. **Gradually Return to the Present Moment**: When your timer rings, don't immediately open your eyes and jump back into your routine. Instead, slowly become aware of your surroundings. Gently wiggle your fingers and toes, and then, when you're ready, slowly open

your eyes.

8. **Practice Regularly**: Consistency is key in meditation. Make it a part of your daily routine. Even a few minutes every day can make a significant difference.

Remember, meditation is not about achieving a certain state, but about being present. It's completely normal for the mind to wander. The practice lies in bringing your attention back, again and again.

Practicing mindfulness meditation regularly can help reduce stress, enhance self-awareness, and improve overall well-being. It's a journey towards understanding and accepting yourself, just as you are.

Chapter Summary

- Modern thinkers have extrapolated on the teachings of ancient philosophers, providing fresh insights relevant to contemporary society.
- Existentialists like Jean-Paul Sartre and Albert Camus focused on individual existence, freedom, and the creation of personal meaning. Sartre's philosophy underscores our freedom and responsibility to create our own life's meaning.
- Psychologists like Carl Jung and Abraham Maslow deepened our understanding of the human psyche. Jung's theories on collective unconsciousness and archetypes broaden our view on human behavior, while Maslow's hierarchy of needs emphasized self-actualization as the pinnacle of human motivation.
- Contemporary spiritual leaders like Eckhart Tolle and Thich Nhat Hanh encourage mindfulness and living in the present moment. Tolle's "Power of Now" emphasizes being present and conscious, and Thich Nhat Hanh

teaches mindful living as a path to peace and joy.

- Modern wisdom complements ancient teachings to provide a comprehensive understanding of ourselves and the world. The philosophies of existentialists and psychologists remind us of our personal freedom and provide tools for navigating our internal world, while modern spiritual leaders guide us towards a mindful, present-focused existence.
- These combined insights from modern thinkers and ancient masters form a rich tapestry of wisdom to guide us in our journey towards self-understanding, fulfillment, and inner peace.

CHAPTER 3

The Stoner Philosophy

Stepping out of the conventional lanes of wisdom, we find ourselves amid a subculture steeped in its unique philosophy—the stoner philosophy. To fully grasp this, we must first understand its historical and cultural context. Stoner philosophy was born from the counterculture movements of the mid-20th century, an era marked by questioning authority, challenging societal norms, and advocating for peace and personal freedom.

The stoner philosophy goes beyond the recreational use of cannabis; it encapsulates a distinctive perspective on life. The essence of this philosophy lies in the pursuit of peace, acceptance, mindfulness, and an alternative lens to perceive reality.

One key principle derived from the stoner perspective is the cultivation of patience. The act of smoking or consuming cannabis requires a deliberate slowing down, a departure from the fast-paced world we inhabit. This slow tempo allows for introspection and reflection, providing space to appreciate the present moment and embrace mindfulness.

The stoner philosophy also champions acceptance and the discarding of judgment. As part of a subculture that has faced societal stigma, stoners understand the value of acceptance and compassion. This ethos extends beyond their community, influencing their interactions with the world, and promoting a more inclusive and accepting worldview.

Additionally, the stoner philosophy encourages us to challenge societal norms and question authority. This questioning is not a call for anarchy, but a critique of blind adherence to societal expectations. It encourages us to step out of societal constructs and view our lives through an unbiased lens, ultimately inspiring us to live a life true to ourselves, not one dictated by external forces.

The wisdom and lessons derived from the stoner perspective are valuable guides in navigating our modern world. The emphasis on mindfulness and patience teaches us to slow down and appreciate the beauty of the present moment. The lessons of acceptance and non-judgment inspire us to be more empathetic and understanding in our interactions with others. The encouragement to challenge norms and question authority pushes us to live authentically, making decisions based on our values and aspirations rather than societal expectations.

In conclusion, the stoner philosophy offers a unique perspective on life, grounded in peace, mindfulness, acceptance, and authenticity. As we continue our quest for wisdom, let us remember these lessons and carry them with us, allowing their gentle whisper to guide us on our path.

Exercise: Letter to Future Self

Writing a letter to your future self is a powerful self-reflection exercise that enables you to gain perspective on your life and see the progress you've made over time. Let's dive into a brief actionable practice on how to go about writing this transformative letter.

1. **Choose Your Future Self's Date**: Decide how far in the future you'd like to write this letter to - it could be one year, five years, or even a decade. Remember, the choice should be

meaningful to you.

2. **Find a Quiet Space**: Choose a quiet, comfortable spot where you can reflect and write without being interrupted.

3. **Reflect on Your Present**: Think about your life in the present moment. What are your hopes, fears, dreams, and challenges? What are the values that you hold dear, and what kind of person do you want to be in the future?

4. **Write the Letter**: Start writing the letter as if you were speaking to a dear friend. Express your thoughts, feelings, aspirations, and worries. It's a letter, so there's no right or wrong format – write from your heart.

5. **Offer Advice**: As you're writing, think about what advice or wisdom you'd like

to offer your future self. This could be a mantra that keeps you grounded, a reminder of your values, or encouragement to pursue your dreams.

6. **Seal and Store the Letter**: Once you've finished, put the letter in an envelope, seal it, and write the date when you're supposed to open it. Store it somewhere safe where you can easily find it in the future.

7. **Open the Letter**: When the date you've written on the envelope arrives, take some time for yourself, open the letter, and read it. Reflect on your journey, the changes, the constants, and see how far you've come.

Writing a letter to your future self can be an emotional, insightful, and liberating exercise. It provides you a snapshot of your past while offering wisdom and perspective to your future self.

Remember, this letter is for you and you alone. It's a personal, private conversation across time, so feel free to express yourself fully and truthfully.

Chapter Summary

- The stoner philosophy emerges from the counterculture movements of the mid-20th century, marked by questioning authority, challenging societal norms, and advocating for personal freedom and peace.
- The philosophy extends beyond the recreational use of cannabis and encapsulates a distinct view of life, emphasizing peace, acceptance, mindfulness, and a unique lens to perceive reality.

- One central principle of the stoner philosophy is the cultivation of patience. The deliberate slowing down associated with cannabis consumption allows for introspection, reflection, and mindfulness.
- Acceptance and the absence of judgment are other fundamental tenets of the stoner philosophy. Stemming from a subculture that faced societal stigma, this perspective values inclusivity and compassion.
- The stoner philosophy encourages questioning societal norms and authority, promoting critical thinking over blind adherence to societal expectations. It urges living authentically, free from undue external influence.
- The teachings of the stoner philosophy—mindfulness, patience, acceptance, non-judgment, and authenticity—offer valuable guidance in navigating modern life, improving interactions with others, and living in alignment with one's values.
- Overall, the stoner philosophy provides a unique lens to view life, emphasizing peace,

mindfulness, acceptance, and authenticity, offering valuable insights for the ongoing quest for wisdom.

CHAPTER 4

Psychedelic Wisdom

As we traverse the labyrinth of human experiences, we occasionally stumble upon a path less traveled. This path, bathed in colors more vivid than we imagined, resonates with sounds more profound than we have heard, and imbued with sensations more intense than we have felt. This is the path of the psychedelic experience, a realm where wisdom isn't acquired from dusty books or scholarly texts but surfaces from the unfathomable depths of the human mind and the boundless expanse of perception.

Psychedelic experiences are as unique and varied as the individuals who dare to embark upon them. They can be deeply personal and introspective, allowing a person to delve into the crevices of their subconscious mind. Or they can be outwardly focused and universal, making the individual feel like a tiny, integral part of the immense cosmos. Despite the wide range of these experiences, there are common themes and lessons that emerge, contributing to a distinctive psychedelic perspective on life.

One of these recurring themes is the sense of interconnectedness. Under the influence of psychedelics, individuals often report the dissolution of self-imposed barriers, leading to a profound sense of unity with the world around them. This isn't a vague philosophical concept but a tangible, experiential reality where the boundaries between self and the universe blur. This newfound sense of oneness fosters a deep-seated appreciation for all life forms and an understanding of the intricate web of existence in which we are all intertwined. It compels us to challenge our rigid, individualistic perspectives, urging us towards greater empathy, compassion, and understanding for other beings and our planet.

Another vital insight from the psychedelic experience is the realization of reality's fluidity. Psychedelics can warp and distort our standard perceptions, revealing that our so-called reality isn't as fixed and objective as we commonly assume. This realization promotes a flexibility in our thinking, encouraging us to remain open to new experiences, perspectives, and possibilities.

Moreover, the psychedelic journey often brings subconscious thoughts, repressed emotions, and latent feelings to the surface of consciousness. This eruption can catalyze deep introspection and rigorous self-analysis, facilitating a journey towards greater self-awareness and personal growth. It's a call to face our deepest fears, confront our buried traumas, and come to terms with our authentic selves.

The wisdom derived from psychedelic experiences offers lessons that can significantly influence our day-to-day existence. The understanding of our interconnectedness with all life forms can inspire us to live with increased empathy, respect, and love. The insight into the fluid nature of reality can open our minds to a broader spectrum of possibilities, fostering adaptability and resilience. The introspection and self-awareness brought about by these experiences can lead to personal growth and authenticity, empowering us to live more fulfilling lives.

In conclusion, the psychedelic journey, though unconventional and often misunderstood, offers a treasure trove of wisdom. However, it's essential to approach these experiences with respect, openness, and curiosity. As we navigate the beautiful complexity of life, let's carry these lessons with us, using them as navigational beacons guiding us towards a life of understanding, compassion, authenticity, and wisdom.

Exercise: Breathwork and Sensory Awareness

Breathwork combined with sensory awareness is a powerful tool that promotes relaxation, reduces stress, and enhances mindfulness. It involves the intentional control of breathing patterns while focusing on the sensory input from your environment. Here's how you can practice this technique.

1. **Find a Comfortable Space**: Choose a location where you won't be disturbed. This could be a quiet room, a garden, or any place where you feel relaxed and safe.

2. **Adopt a Comfortable Posture**: You can sit, lie down, or even stand, as long as you're comfortable. Ensure your back is straight and relaxed.

3. **Close Your Eyes**: Gently close your eyes to help sharpen your other senses.

4. **Focus on Your Breath**: Pay attention to your breath as it flows in and out. Don't try to control it; just observe its natural rhythm.

5. **Deepen Your Breath**: Slowly start to breathe more deeply, filling your lungs fully on each inhale and emptying them completely on each exhale. Count to four on each in-breath, hold for a count of four, exhale for a count of four, then wait for a count of four before inhaling again.

6. **Engage Your Senses**: Now, start to shift your attention from your breath to your senses. What do you hear? What do you feel? Is there any taste in your mouth? Can you smell anything?

Engage with each sense one by one.

7. **Rotate Your Attention**: Spend a minute or two on each sense before moving to the next. Cycle through them several times, fully immersing yourself in each sensory experience.

8. **Return to Your Breath**: After you've spent some time with your senses, gently bring your attention back to your breath. Notice if it has changed during the practice.

9. **Open Your Eyes**: When you're ready, slowly open your eyes and bring your awareness back to the room.

Remember, this is your practice. If at any point it feels uncomfortable, or you become overwhelmed, return your focus to your breath or open your eyes. With regular practice, this exercise can increase your mindfulness, improve your stress response, and enhance your overall well-being.

Chapter Summary

- Psychedelic experiences offer a unique path to wisdom, illuminating insights from the depths of the human mind and the expanse of perception.
- These experiences can be personal and introspective or outwardly focused and universal, each contributing to a unique psychedelic perspective on life.
- A recurrent theme in psychedelic experiences is the sense of interconnectedness, leading to a profound appreciation for all life forms and a deeper understanding of our place in the cosmos.
- Psychedelics often reveal the fluidity of reality, challenging our standard perceptions and

encouraging openness to new experiences, perspectives, and possibilities.

- The psychedelic journey can bring subconscious thoughts, repressed emotions, and latent feelings to conscious awareness, promoting introspection, self-awareness, and personal growth.
- The insights derived from these experiences—interconnectedness, fluid reality, and introspection—can influence our daily lives, inspiring empathy, adaptability, and personal authenticity.
- Despite its unconventional nature, the psychedelic journey offers a trove of wisdom when approached with respect, openness, and curiosity, serving as a guide towards a life of understanding, compassion, and authenticity.

CHAPTER 5

The Interplay of Ancient and Modern Wisdom

In the grand panorama of human knowledge, wisdom weaves a tapestry where threads of antiquity intertwine harmoniously with those of the present age. This dance of ancient and modern wisdom creates a rich mosaic of insights, providing us with an encompassing guide to navigate the complexities of life. The distinct attributes of both ancient and modern wisdom complement each other, and when considered together, they present a holistic lens through which we can understand our world.

Ancient wisdom, deeply rooted in cultures and philosophies that have endured the relentless passage of time, offers a sturdy foundation on which we can build our understanding. Consider the teachings of ancient masters such as Buddha, Lao Tzu, and Socrates. Their profound insights into the human condition, articulated centuries ago, resonate with us even today. They extol virtues such as mindfulness, compassion, moderation, and the relentless pursuit of truth. Despite their antiquity, these principles are relevant today and serve as unswerving beacons guiding us through the choppy seas of our ever-evolving world.

On the other hand, modern wisdom represents the evolving understanding of ourselves and the universe we inhabit. It reflects the nuanced complexities of our contemporary world, providing fresh insights into age-old problems. Modern thinkers, including the likes of Jean-Paul Sartre and Albert

Camus, challenge us to carve our own meaning out of the block of existence. Psychologists like Carl Jung and Abraham Maslow provide us with tools to explore our inner worlds. Contemporary spiritual guides, such as Eckhart Tolle and Thich Nhat Hanh, advocate for mindfulness and presence amidst the maelstrom of our fast-paced world.

Drawing a comparison between ancient and modern wisdom, we find that they address the same fundamental human inquiries but from different vantage points. Ancient wisdom often promotes living harmoniously, in accordance with nature and the immutable laws of the universe. In contrast, modern wisdom emphasizes individuality, authenticity, and personal freedom, encouraging us to script our own narratives.

The amalgamation of ancient and modern wisdom forms an invaluable guide for our daily lives. They jointly advocate for mindfulness, authenticity, compassion, and the pursuit of understanding. The timeless principles espoused by ancient wisdom offer a stable bedrock in an era marked by rapid change.

Concurrently, the emphasis of modern wisdom on individuality and authenticity empowers us to shape our own destinies and live true to our inner selves.

In conclusion, the dance of ancient and modern wisdom creates a symphony that resonates with depth and nuance. Each contributes unique melodies, and when harmonized, they provide a comprehensive guide for navigating the labyrinth of the modern world. As we continue to tread our paths, let these pearls of wisdom light our way, guiding us towards a life rich in understanding, authenticity, and compassion.

Exercise: Body Scan Meditation

A body scan meditation is a mindfulness practice designed to promote greater awareness of the physical body. It works by systematically focusing on different regions of the body, from the toes to the head, and noting any sensations, feelings, or thoughts that arise. Here is how you can practice a body scan meditation.

1. **Find a Comfortable Space**: Choose a quiet and comfortable location where you won't be disturbed for the duration of the practice.

2. **Position Your Body**: Lie down on your back if possible. If you can't, find a seated position that's comfortable. Ensure your body is relaxed and your posture is natural.

3. **Close Your Eyes**: Close your eyes gently to minimize external distractions and focus inward.

4. **Take a Few Deep Breaths**: Breathe in deeply, hold for a few seconds, and then breathe out slowly. Repeat this a few

times to center your mind.

5. **Start the Body Scan**: Begin the scan at your toes. Take note of any sensation you might feel, such as tingling, warmth, coolness, tension, or relaxation. Remember, there's no need to change anything. Just observe.

6. **Move Slowly Up Your Body**: Continue the scan up through your feet, ankles, lower legs, knees, and so on. Take your time and pay attention to each part before moving on to the next.

7. **Observe Without Judgment**: Throughout the scan, it's crucial to maintain an attitude of non-judgmental observation. If you notice discomfort or tension, simply acknowledge it without trying to change it.

8. **Acknowledge Your Thoughts**: It's natural for thoughts to arise during this meditation. When they do, simply acknowledge them and return your focus to the body scan.

9. **Complete the Scan**: Continue the scan until you reach the top of your head. Take a moment to observe the body as a whole.

10. **Return to Awareness**: When you're ready, slowly open your eyes and bring your awareness back to the room.

This practice can be done for as short as five minutes or as long as an hour—it's flexible to your needs. Regular practice of body scan meditation can enhance body awareness, promote relaxation, and reduce stress.

Chapter Summary

- The interplay of ancient and modern wisdom creates a comprehensive guide for understanding life, with ancient wisdom offering a sturdy foundation and modern wisdom reflecting our evolving understanding.
- Ancient wisdom, derived from teachings of masters like Buddha, Lao Tzu, and Socrates, extols virtues like mindfulness, compassion, and truth-seeking, serving as timeless guides in our changing world.
- Modern wisdom, represented by thinkers like Sartre, Camus, Jung, Maslow, Tolle, and Thich Nhat Hanh, challenges us to create our own meaning, explore our inner worlds, and practice mindfulness and presence.
- While ancient wisdom promotes harmony with nature and universal laws, modern wisdom emphasizes individuality, authenticity, and personal freedom.
- The combination of ancient and modern wisdom promotes mindfulness, authenticity,

compassion, and understanding in our daily lives.

- Ancient wisdom provides stability in times of rapid change, while modern wisdom empowers us to.

CHAPTER 6

From Stoner Insight to Psychedelic Wisdom

Transitioning from mere stoner insights to the profound realm of psychedelic wisdom involves a journey of introspection that demands not just courage but also mindfulness, respect, and openness. This less traveled path, studded with the jewels of profound wisdom, is not a course for the casually curious. Instead, it's a transformative voyage designed for the seekers of profound wisdom and the explorers of inner realms. In this chapter, we will delve into the roadmap for navigating this transformative journey.

Before you embark on this psychedelic odyssey, mindful preparation is of paramount importance. The act of creating a safe, serene, and comforting environment—a concept known as the "setting"—lays the groundwork for the journey. Furthermore, preparing oneself mentally for the journey, or the "set," is an integral part of this initial phase. A significant part of this mental preparation involves setting an intention. This intention could be a question you seek answers to, an area of your life you wish to gain a deeper understanding of, or an aspect of your personality you wish to explore during the psychedelic experience. This process isn't about entering the experience with a rigid set of expectations, but rather, it's about approaching the experience with an open mind, a receptacle ready to receive the teachings the journey may offer.

Venturing into the psychedelic realm can be akin to navigating through a dreamlike landscape, a dimension teeming with vibrant colors, profound insights, and a kaleidoscope of complex emotions. While on this journey, it is critical to remember to maintain your breath, remain open, and surrender to the unfolding experience. Resisting the ebb and flow of this psychedelic tide can result in discomfort and fear, while acceptance can pave the way for a smoother journey, akin to flowing with the current of a river.

Several practical strategies can be beneficial for navigating the psychedelic terrain. When the journey seems overwhelming, employing grounding techniques can provide a sense of stability. This could mean focusing on the rhythm of your breath, feeling the comforting weight of your body pressing against the ground, or simply reminding yourself that you've consumed a substance and will inevitably return to your usual state of consciousness.

Arguably the most challenging yet immensely rewarding aspect of the psychedelic journey is the integration phase. This involves distilling the insights and lessons gleaned from the journey and applying them to your everyday life. Journaling your experiences and insights immediately following the journey can be invaluable. Revisiting these notes frequently helps in the process of translating psychedelic wisdom into actionable steps in your life. This act of translation may trigger changes in behavior, attitude, or perspectives, thereby serving as a catalyst for personal growth.

Psychedelic wisdom can be an exceptionally powerful tool for personal growth and transformation. It can help us transcend the confines of our everyday patterns, opening us up to new ways of perceiving and being. However, it is of utmost importance to remember that these substances are merely tools, not panaceas. They hold the potential to unlock doors, but the responsibility to step through and initiate lasting changes rests solely upon us.

In conclusion, the evolution from stoner insight to psychedelic wisdom represents a profound process of transformation. By adopting mindful preparation, respectful navigation, and dedicated integration, we can effectively harness this wisdom. This can significantly enhance our lives, fostering an environment ripe for growth, understanding, and profound transformation.

Exercise: Yoga Nidra (Guided Relaxation)

Yoga Nidra, often referred to as "yogic sleep," is a guided relaxation technique rooted in the ancient practices of yoga. It invites you to a state of deep relaxation, yet one in which you remain conscious and aware. Here's a brief guide on how to practice Yoga Nidra.

1. **Prepare Your Space**: Select a quiet, comfortable area where you won't be disturbed. Lay down a yoga mat or blanket, and consider having a pillow for your head and a blanket to cover yourself, as body temperature can drop

during deep relaxation.

2. **Lie Down**: Lay down flat on your back in a position known as Shavasana, or corpse pose. Position your feet hip-width apart, allow your toes to fall outwards, and rest your hands by your sides with palms facing up. If lying flat is uncomfortable, you can bend your knees or elevate your legs on a bolster or cushion.

3. **Close Your Eyes**: Gently close your eyes, signaling to your body that it's time to turn inwards and begin the process of relaxation.

4. **Take a Few Deep Breaths**: Take a few moments to focus on your breath, feeling each inhalation and exhalation. Notice the rise and fall of your abdomen, the sensation of air entering and leaving

your nostrils.

5. **Set an Intention (Sankalpa)**: Yoga Nidra traditionally begins with setting a simple, positive intention or Sankalpa. This could be a short affirmation in the present tense, such as "I am at peace," "I am healthy," or "I love myself." Repeat it mentally a few times with conviction.

6. **Follow the Guide**: Whether you're following a recorded script or a live instructor, surrender to the guide. You'll be led to move your awareness to different parts of your body, encouraged to visualize various images, and asked to notice sensations, thoughts, and feelings.

7. **Return to Consciousness**: Typically, the guided Yoga Nidra practice will end by gradually bringing you back to your

full consciousness and physical surroundings. Take a few deep breaths, wiggle your fingers and toes, and slowly open your eyes.

8. **Notice How You Feel**: Before jumping up and returning to activity, spend a few moments noticing how you feel. Observe any changes in your physical, emotional, and mental state.

Yoga Nidra is a practice of deep rest and relaxation that can be profoundly rejuvenating. Remember, there's no right or wrong experience in Yoga Nidra. Each experience is unique to the individual.

Chapter Summary

- Transitioning from stoner insights to psychedelic wisdom is a journey that requires mindfulness, respect, and openness.
- Before embarking on this journey, one must prepare mindfully, including creating a safe and comfortable environment ("setting") and mental preparation ("set").
- Setting an intention for the psychedelic experience can help guide the journey and yield meaningful insights.
- Navigating the psychedelic realm can feel overwhelming, but remembering to breathe, stay open, and surrender to the experience is vital.
- Using grounding techniques can help manage overwhelming sensations during the journey.
- The integration phase, where insights and lessons from the psychedelic experience are applied to everyday life, is crucial for personal growth.
- Journaling the experiences and insights can aid in the integration process.
- Psychedelic wisdom can be a potent tool for personal transformation, helping to break

everyday patterns and open up new ways of being and perceiving.

- While psychedelics can unlock doors to new insights, it's important to remember that they are tools, not solutions—it is up to the individual to make lasting changes in their lives.
- Mindful preparation, respectful navigation, and dedicated integration are the keys to successfully transitioning from stoner insight to psychedelic wisdom.

CHAPTER 7

Life Lessons from the Masters

When it comes to wisdom, life lessons abound. They can be found in the teachings of ancient sages, the theories of modern philosophers, and the contemplations of unconventional thinkers from psychedelic explorers to stoner philosophers. These pearls of wisdom, though scattered across different eras and cultures, all have the potential to guide us through life's complexities and illuminate the path to joy, fulfillment, and inner peace.

Let us first journey back to ancient times, where wisdom was sought from introspection, observation of nature, and philosophical discourse. Figures like Buddha, Lao Tzu, and Socrates are still revered for their timeless wisdom. Buddha's Middle Way encourages us to embrace moderation and balance in all aspects of life, a teaching that remains relevant in our fast-paced, consumer-driven world. Lao Tzu, with his Taoist philosophy, inspires us to seek simplicity, live in tune with nature's rhythm, and appreciate the quietude amidst life's clamor. Socrates, the revered Greek philosopher, believed that 'an unexamined life is not worth living,' prompting us towards introspection, self-awareness, and constant learning.

As we move forward in time, modern masters offer wisdom that resonates with our current era's intricacies. Existentialists like Jean-Paul Sartre and Albert Camus implore us to recognize our inherent freedom, to take responsibility for our destiny, and to create our own purpose in a seemingly meaningless universe. Renowned psychologists such as Carl Jung remind us of the importance of understanding our inner psyche, advocating for introspection and the integration of our darker, often neglected aspects, known as the shadow self. Contemporary mindfulness practitioners like Jon Kabat-Zinn highlight the transformative power of living in the present moment, fostering a sense of peace and tranquility amid life's turbulence.

Turning towards more unconventional sources, the laid-back philosophies of stoner culture and the profound insights from psychedelic explorations offer a unique perspective. Stoner philosophy urges us to question the status quo, to remain curious, and to approach life with a sense of wonder. Psychedelic wisdom, on the other hand, takes us on a deep dive into the subconscious, unraveling profound truths about ourselves, our interconnectedness, and our place within the cosmos.

Integrating these wisdom-filled life lessons into our daily lives requires effort and introspection. Start by reflecting on each teaching, assessing its relevance and applicability to your personal circumstances. Techniques like journaling, meditation, and mindful contemplation can assist in this internalization process. As these lessons become ingrained within your psyche, they begin to influence your actions, decision-making process, and overall outlook on life, serving as a compass guiding you towards wisdom, peace, and fulfillment.

However, it's important to remember that these teachings are not rigid doctrines but flexible guiding principles, intended to be tailored to your personal journey and unique experiences. They offer various routes on the map of life, but the choice of path and how you navigate it ultimately lies in your hands. Embrace this wisdom, intricately weave it into the fabric of your life, and watch as your journey unfolds towards deeper understanding, enduring peace, and abiding joy.

Exercise: Compassion

Compassion is a powerful emotion that fosters connection, empathy, and understanding. Cultivating compassion can significantly enrich our lives and the lives of those around us. The following exercise is a simple yet impactful practice to cultivate compassion.

1. **Select a Person**: Begin by choosing someone in your life. It could be a close loved one, a neutral acquaintance, or even someone with whom you have difficulties.

2. **Reflect on Their Humanity**: Take a few moments to consider that this person, like you, has aspirations, hopes, fears, and struggles. They experience joy, sorrow, love, and loss. They are human, just as you are.

3. **Reflect on Their Desire for Happiness**: Recognize that this person, just like you, seeks happiness and wishes to avoid suffering. Reflect on this shared human experience and desire.

4. **Generate Feelings of Compassion**: Now, with these reflections in mind, try to generate feelings of compassion towards this person. You might imagine sending them warmth, kindness, or a wish for their wellbeing.

5. **Repeat with Other Individuals**: Repeat this exercise with different people in your life. As your comfort with the practice grows, try extending your compassion to more challenging individuals or even to all beings.

6. **Reflect on the Experience**: After you finish the exercise, spend a few

moments reflecting on the experience. How did it make you feel? Did you notice any changes in your feelings towards the individuals?

Remember, like any other skill, cultivating compassion requires consistent practice. However, with time and patience, it can significantly enhance your ability to connect with others and foster a greater sense of peace and happiness within yourself.

Chapter Summary

- Ancient wisdom, from figures like Buddha, Lao Tzu, and Socrates, teaches us moderation, mindfulness, living in harmony with nature, and the importance of introspection and self-awareness.
- Modern thinkers like Jean-Paul Sartre, Albert Camus, and Carl Jung encourage us to

acknowledge our inherent freedom, create our own purpose, and understand our inner psyche. Jon Kabat-Zinn emphasizes the transformative power of mindfulness and being present.

- Unconventional wisdom from stoner philosophy and psychedelic explorations inspire us to question the status quo, stay curious, and understand our interconnectedness and place within the cosmos.
- To effectively apply these lessons, it's important to reflect on each teaching, understand its relevance to personal life, and internalize it through journaling, meditation, and mindful contemplation.
- These teachings should be seen as flexible guiding principles, rather than rigid doctrines, to be adapted to personal circumstances and experiences. They provide possible routes for navigating life but leave the journey's details up to the individual.
- Embracing these pearls of wisdom and integrating them into one's life can lead to a

deeper understanding, enduring peace, and abiding joy.

CHAPTER 8

Unifying Love

Universal love—a concept as profound as it is timeless. It is a love that defies boundaries, transcends differences, and unifies us in a grand cosmic tapestry. It is an enduring truth found in wisdom traditions across time and culture, serving as a testament to our shared humanity. This chapter aims to delve into the concept of universal love and explore how it threads through ancient and modern wisdom, stoner philosophy, and psychedelic experiences.

Ancient philosophies hold a treasure trove of insights into the nature of universal love. In the Hellenic world, the Greek philosophers spoke of 'Agape,' an unconditional love that transcends personal relations and embraces all humanity. Meanwhile, the Eastern traditions have their unique perspectives. Buddhism propounds the practice of 'Metta,' or loving-kindness, which extends empathy and goodwill to all sentient beings. Similarly, the Hindu philosophy of 'Bhakti' underscores a passionate devotion to the divine, expressed through acts of love.

In the realm of modern thought, love remains a subject of profound inquiry. The existentialist philosopher Jean-Paul Sartre touched upon the concept of 'authentic love.' This love is one that acknowledges the independence and freedom of the other, steering clear of possession. Further, the field of psychology has also contributed to our understanding of love. Carl Rogers, an influential psychologist, emphasized 'unconditional positive regard' in therapeutic relationships, a form of non-judgmental, accepting love.

Emerging from the haze of stoner philosophy and the colorful vistas of psychedelic wisdom, the exploration of love takes on a more experiential form. Users often report a heightened sense of empathy, interconnectedness, and a profound realization of universal love during their experiences with cannabis or psychedelics. These states of altered consciousness can dissolve perceived barriers between the self and others, fostering a profound sense of shared love.

So, how can we cultivate this universal love in our daily lives? It all starts with the self. Self-love is the foundational bedrock upon which we build our capacity to love others. By acknowledging and cherishing our inherent worth, we learn to extend the same appreciation towards others. Mindfulness and meditation can serve as powerful tools to foster empathy and compassion. Techniques such as Loving-Kindness Meditation (Metta Bhavana) can be particularly effective in nurturing feelings of universal love.

The wisdom from stoner and psychedelic experiences can also be harnessed to cultivate this boundless love. Reflecting upon and integrating the feelings of unity and interconnectedness experienced during these altered states can nurture a deep sense of universal love. Such reflection can transform ephemeral experiences into lasting changes in perspective.

In conclusion, universal love is more than an abstract concept—it is a unifying force that bridges cultures, philosophies, and individual experiences. Whether through the lens of ancient sages, modern thinkers, or the psychedelic voyager, the message is clear: universal love is the fabric that binds us all. Cultivating this love within ourselves allows us to contribute to a more compassionate, empathetic, and loving world, one heartbeat at a time.

Exercise: Nature Connection

Connecting with nature can be a profound and transformative experience. It can foster a sense of peace, enhance mindfulness, and provide a deep sense of belonging. Here is a simple yet effective exercise to help you connect with nature.

1. **Find a Natural Setting**: Choose a location in nature where you feel safe and comfortable. This could be a park, a forest, a beach, or even your backyard garden.

2. **Sensory Immersion**: Spend some time immersing yourself in the environment using all your senses. Listen to the sounds, observe the sights, smell the scents, touch the textures, and if safe, taste something like a fresh berry.

3. **Mindful Observation**: Pick a natural object in your vicinity—a leaf, a stone, a stream—and spend some time observing it mindfully. Notice its details, its textures, its colors.

4. **Gratitude Practice**: Take a moment to express gratitude for the natural world around you. Recognize the interdependence of all life forms and express thanks for their contribution to your life.

5. **Reflect and Journal**: After the exercise, spend some time reflecting on your experience. You may choose to journal about it—what did you notice? How did you feel?

By consciously taking the time to connect with nature, we can foster a deeper sense of connection with the world around us, promoting mental wellbeing, peace, and an elevated appreciation for our environment.

Chapter Summary

- Universal love, an essential concept in various philosophies and wisdom traditions, bridges cultures and individual experiences.
- Ancient Greek philosophy introduces 'Agape,' a form of love that encompasses all humanity, while Eastern philosophies highlight 'Metta' and 'Bhakti,' promoting empathy and divine devotion.
- Modern philosophers and psychologists, like Jean-Paul Sartre and Carl Rogers, explore notions of 'authentic love' and 'unconditional positive regard,' emphasizing respect for individual freedom and non-judgmental acceptance.
- Stoner philosophy and psychedelic wisdom provide experiential insights into love, often

leading to heightened empathy, interconnectedness, and a deep sense of universal love.

- Cultivating universal love begins with self-love, extending this love towards others through mindfulness, meditation, and practices like Loving-Kindness Meditation.
- Insights and experiences from stoner and psychedelic journeys can be reflected upon and integrated into daily life, nurturing a profound sense of universal love.
- Embracing universal love contributes to a more compassionate, empathetic, and loving world.

CHAPTER 9

Creating Harmonious Living

Crafting a harmonious life represents the elegant artistry of balance, a sophisticated waltz between acceptance and action, self-awareness and comprehension, giving and receiving. The profound wisdom distilled from various philosophies, when alloyed with insights derived from stoner musings and psychedelic journeys, serves as our compass, guiding us towards the delicate equilibrium conducive to a life of harmony.

By applying the teachings of diverse philosophies, we can directly address the primary disruptors of harmony in our lives: stress, conflict, and disconnection. Stoicism, the timeless philosophy embraced by ancient Greeks and Romans, offers invaluable lessons on maintaining tranquility amid life's turbulence. It guides us to discern the things within our control from those beyond our grasp and encourages us to relinquish our hold on the latter. Adopting this perspective equips us with tools to mitigate stress, empowering us to maintain balance even in adversity's face.

Conflict, a potent disruptor of harmony, can be effectively managed by incorporating the principles of the Eastern philosophy of Taoism. By advocating flexibility and adaptability, Taoism gently guides us to flow with life's circumstances, thereby diminishing friction and fostering tranquility. The Taoist principle of Yin and Yang underscores the importance of embracing duality, illuminating that opposing forces aren't necessarily conflicting, but rather elements that contribute to equilibrium.

Disconnection, a sense of being adrift from our true selves and others around us, can be healed through insights gleaned from modern psychology and stoner philosophy. Carl Jung's teachings emphasize the significance of self-integration, which aids in attuning to our inner world, thereby fostering personal harmony. Stoner philosophy, renowned for championing interconnectedness and empathy, can be instrumental in nurturing our relationships with others, thereby promoting social harmony.

Let's delve into the transformative journeys of individuals who have successfully integrated these philosophies into their lives. Consider Alice, a high-powered lawyer persistently beleaguered by stress. Her life took a positive turn when she discovered Stoic philosophy, and by separating her reactions from external events, she succeeded in significantly diminishing her stress levels. Then there's Jack, a talented musician whose interactions with his bandmates were frequently marred by disagreements. Inspired by Taoist philosophy, he adopted a more flexible approach, amicably resolving conflicts and fostering a harmonious band environment. Reflect on Emma's story, a college student plagued by feelings of disconnection from her peers. Guided by mindful cannabis use and introspective reflection, she cultivated deeper empathy and understanding, which led her to form meaningful connections.

These real-life accounts vividly illustrate that philosophy transcends intellectual engagement to serve as a practical toolkit for life. The wisdom handed down by ancient sages, the insights of modern thinkers, and the revelations from stoner and psychedelic experiences—all these provide invaluable resources to cultivate harmony in our lives. As we internalize and integrate these teachings into our daily lives, we inch closer to a life characterized by greater peace, joy, and harmony.

Exercise: Walking Meditation

Walking meditation is a simple yet powerful mindfulness practice that can be integrated into your daily routine. It allows you to connect your physical movement with your mental and emotional state, encouraging deep awareness and relaxation. Here is a step-by-step guide to practicing walking meditation.

1. **Choose a Suitable Location**: Find a quiet and peaceful place where you can walk undisturbed for a few minutes. This could be a tranquil part of your home, a garden, or a park.

2. **Start with Stillness**: Before you begin walking, stand still for a moment. Close your eyes and take a few deep breaths, centering yourself in the present moment.

3. **Begin to Walk Slowly**: Start walking at a slower pace than usual. Keep your eyes open but let your gaze be soft, not focused on anything in particular.

4. **Pay Attention to Your Steps**: Notice every aspect of the action of walking. Feel your feet making contact with the ground, the sensation of your legs moving, and the rhythm of your steps.

5. **Be Mindful of Your Surroundings**: As you continue to walk, become mindful of your environment. Notice the sounds, smells, and sensations around you. However, keep your primary focus on your steps.

6. **Gently Return Your Focus**: If your mind wanders, gently bring your focus back to your steps. This is a practice of mindfulness and patience.

7. **Conclude Your Walk**: After 10-15 minutes, or a duration that suits you, gradually bring your walking meditation to a close. Stand still for a moment, acknowledging the transition from walking meditation to your routine.

Walking meditation is a flexible practice that can be adapted to suit your needs and circumstances. It can be a bridge between formal meditation practice and everyday mindfulness, helping you bring a deeper sense of awareness into your daily life.

Chapter Summary

- The path to harmony is a dance between acceptance and action, self-awareness and understanding, and giving and receiving.

- Stoicism teaches us to differentiate between what's in our control and what's not, helping to manage stress.
- Taoism promotes flexibility and adaptability, fostering peace by reducing conflict.
- Taoist philosophy also encourages embracing duality, contributing to balance.
- Disconnection can be addressed by integrating Carl Jung's teachings about self-awareness and the stoner philosophy's emphasis on empathy and interconnectedness.
- Real-life examples show how these philosophical teachings can be used to foster harmony in various life situations.
- The wisdom of ancient and modern philosophies, combined with stoner and psychedelic insights, provides a toolkit for creating a harmonious life.

CHAPTER 10

Pathways to Lasting Happiness

One could argue that the pursuit of happiness is one of humanity's most fervent quests, often dominating our life decisions and paths. Indeed, it forms the bedrock of many philosophical discourses, theories of psychology, and individual aspirations that span the ages. By knitting together the wisdom of time-tested philosophies, the insights derived from contemporary psychological understanding, and the profound enlightenment that stoner and psychedelic experiences often bring, we can navigate the landscape of life with a roadmap to lasting happiness.

Turning the pages back to the era of ancient wisdom, the philosophy of Epicureanism springs forth with lessons of profound relevance. Epicureans prized simplicity, extolling the virtues of 'ataraxia,' a tranquil state of existence devoid of distress and devoid of fear. In today's world, marked by a seemingly unending quest for material accumulation, this ancient philosophy shines a beacon on a different path – one where happiness is sought not in the pursuit of more but in the simple enjoyment and appreciation of what one already possesses.

As we journey from the old world into the realm of modern psychology, we encounter the burgeoning field of positive psychology. This scientific study of human flourishing underscores the pivotal role of character strengths, nurturing relationships, meaningful pursuits, and a sense of accomplishment in fashioning a life of happiness. The focus shifts from repairing our weaknesses to harnessing and augmenting our strengths, thereby cultivating a fertile soil from which well-being and enduring happiness can bloom.

Contributing to this discourse, stoner philosophy and psychedelic wisdom bring in valuable insights often overlooked in conventional discourses. These unique experiences provide a deep dive into our subconscious, fostering an enhanced sense of self-awareness, peace, and contentment. Psychedelic experiences, in particular, have been known to catalyze profound revelations about our interconnectedness with the cosmos, igniting a sense of purpose and amplifying happiness.

So, how do we tend this garden of joy and peace? Firstly, through the practice of gratitude. Recognizing and appreciating the blessings we already have seeds the ground for contentment and happiness. Secondly, the cultivation of mindfulness enhances our ability to engage with the present moment, amplifying the joy found in our daily experiences. Thirdly, fostering meaningful connections with others nurtures the roots of our happiness, as strong, positive relationships contribute significantly to our overall well-being.

Strategies such as reflective journaling can assist us in integrating the insights gleaned from stoner or psychedelic experiences, enabling them to percolate into our daily lives. This practice of mindful reflection can foster self-awareness, catalyze personal growth, and ultimately create an environment conducive to lasting happiness.

In the final analysis, it's essential to bear in mind that happiness is not a static destination to be reached. Rather, it is a dynamic journey to be embarked upon. It demands continual effort, self-compassion, and patience. As we traverse the landscape of life, weaving together the threads of philosophical wisdom, psychological insights, and experiential learning, we construct our unique tapestry of lasting happiness.

Exercise: My Ideal Day

The 'My Ideal Day' writing exercise is an effective tool to gain clarity about your values, goals, and priorities. By visualizing and describing your perfect day, you can identify what truly matters to you and start taking steps to make it a reality. Here is a step-by-step guide on how to conduct this exercise.

1. **Set Aside Time**: Find a quiet space and time where you won't be disturbed. Allow yourself at least 30 minutes to fully engage in this exercise.

2. **Ground Yourself**: Take a few moments to settle your mind. You might find it helpful to take a few deep breaths or do a brief mindfulness exercise to center yourself.

3. **Start Writing**: Begin to describe your

ideal day. Start from the moment you wake up to when you go to sleep. Be as specific as possible. Detail where you are, who you're with, what you're doing, how you're feeling, and why these elements are important to you.

4. **Be Realistic Yet Optimistic**: This exercise isn't about crafting a day that's impossible or based purely on fantasy. Make it aspirational yet feasible. It should inspire you but also be something you can start working towards.

5. **Review Your Ideal Day**: Once you've written out your ideal day, read it back to yourself. Pay attention to the elements that make this day 'ideal' for you. These can give you insight into what values and activities truly make you happy and satisfied.

6. **Take Action**: After identifying the elements of your ideal day, consider what small steps you could take to make your current reality closer to this ideal. You might not be able to achieve everything in one go, but every little step can make a big difference.

Remember, your 'Ideal Day' is not set in stone. As you grow and evolve, so will your vision of an ideal day. Regularly revisit this exercise to keep your goals and priorities in tune with your personal growth.

Chapter Summary

- The pursuit of happiness, a universal human endeavor, is explored across ancient and modern philosophies, psychological theories, and personal experiences.

- Epicureanism emphasizes the significance of simple pleasures and 'ataraxia,' a tranquil state of existence free from fear and distress.
- Positive psychology underlines the importance of harnessing character strengths, fostering relationships, and pursuing meaningful endeavors to promote happiness.
- Stoner philosophy and psychedelic experiences contribute to understanding happiness by fostering self-awareness, peace, and a sense of interconnectedness.
- Daily practices such as expressing gratitude, practicing mindfulness, and building meaningful connections can foster lasting happiness.
- Strategies like reflective journaling can assist in integrating insights from stoner or psychedelic experiences, fostering self-awareness and personal growth.
- Happiness is not a static destination but a dynamic journey requiring consistent effort, self-compassion, and patience.

- Weaving together wisdom from different philosophies and experiences, we can carve our unique path to lasting happiness.

CONCLUSION

Embracing the Journey - Future Pathways of Wisdom and Insight

As our voyage into varied wisdoms and insights, ancient to contemporary and sober to stoned, comes full circle, we find ourselves not at the final destination but rather on the threshold of a new beginning. A journey enriched by profound understanding, heightened self-awareness, and an ever-deepening engagement with life's manifold experiences awaits us. We stand on the precipice of a path leading toward a harmonious existence, universal love, inner peace, and sustainable happiness.

In our quest, we have woven together a comprehensive tapestry of wisdom. It has become clear that wisdom and understanding are not the exclusive domains of any single philosophy, discipline, or personal experience. Instead, they emerge from a confluence of multiple perspectives, each adding unique pieces to the complex puzzle of existence. Ancient wisdom provides timeless truths, while modern insights offer contextual understanding, together forming a robust framework that helps us navigate the tumultuous seas of life with heightened skill and wisdom.

In this extensive mosaic of knowledge, stoner philosophy and psychedelic experiences hold a special place. They serve as potent lenses, piercing through the veneer of ordinary perception to reveal the deeper strata of reality and consciousness. They give us access to uncharted territories within our minds, fostering profound moments of self-discovery and catalyzing transformative personal growth.

As we assimilate these wisdoms and insights into our everyday lives, we begin to notice that they don't just illuminate the path to happiness, but redefine our very conception of happiness itself. They teach us that happiness is not a static endpoint, a prize to be won at life's end. Instead, it's a dynamic state of being, a constant companion evolving and maturing alongside us as we traverse our life's journey.

The future pathways of wisdom and insight are infinite, only bound by the scope of our eagerness to explore, learn, and grow. The continuous discourse between various philosophies, the harmonious convergence of science and spirituality, and the growing acceptance of stoner and psychedelic experiences as instruments for personal growth—all these elements are paving the way for an exciting future for wisdom and insight seekers.

So, let's embrace this journey wholeheartedly. Each fleeting moment, every unique experience, and every nugget of insight we unearth is a stepping stone on our singular path of self-discovery and understanding. It's crucial to remember that the journey matters far more than the destination. The pursuit of wisdom and insight, in itself, is a profound source of joy, fulfillment, and growth. Remember to enjoy the process as you set forth on this remarkable quest.

Exercise: Intention Setting

Setting intentions is a powerful practice that can guide you towards fulfilling your personal and professional goals. It involves defining what you wish to achieve or cultivate and directing your mental energy towards these aims. Here is a step-by-step guide to effectively set your intentions.

1. **Find a Quiet Space**: Select a place where you can focus without distractions. This will help you concentrate and align your thoughts towards your goals.

2. **Ground Yourself**: Before setting your intentions, it is important to clear your mind. Engage in a short mindfulness exercise, such as deep breathing, to create a calm mental state.

3. **Reflect on What You Desire**: Consider what you truly want in different areas of your life such as personal growth, relationships, career, and health. Think about what success looks like for you in these areas.

4. **Write Down Your Intentions**: Start writing your intentions, phrasing them in the present tense as if they are already

happening. For example, instead of writing "I want to be more patient," write "I am becoming more patient each day." This helps in embedding your intentions into your subconscious mind.

5. **Make Your Intentions Actionable**: Create intentions that lead to concrete actions. For example, if your intention is to cultivate more patience, your related action could be "When I feel impatient, I will take three deep breaths before responding."

6. **Regularly Revisit Your Intentions**: Make a habit of reviewing your intentions daily. Visualizing them each day can reinforce your commitment and drive action.

Remember, intention setting is not about immediate perfection but continual growth and evolution. Be kind to yourself as you embark on this journey of intentional living.

Chapter Summary

- Our exploration of wisdom and insights culminates not in an end but a beginning, marked by deeper understanding, greater self-awareness, and a richer life experience.
- Wisdom and understanding emerge from a confluence of various philosophies and experiences, each contributing its unique insight.
- Stoner philosophy and psychedelic experiences provide a distinctive lens for understanding reality and consciousness, fostering self-discovery and personal growth.
- These wisdoms and insights not only guide us towards happiness but also reshape our understanding of happiness as a dynamic state of being.

- The future of wisdom and insight lies in the ongoing dialogue between different philosophies, the convergence of science and spirituality, and the growing acceptance of stoner and psychedelic experiences as tools for personal growth.
- Each moment, experience, and insight on this journey is a stepping stone on our unique path of self-discovery and understanding.
- The pursuit of wisdom and insight, in itself, is a profound source of joy, fulfillment, and growth

AUTHOR BIO

Orion Myst, although a moniker, resonates with the unique and transformative journey of a man who has spent his life exploring the realms of spirituality and self-discovery. Though his formal education was in a Catholic school, Orion found himself drawn to the enigmatic world of ritual and metaphysics early in life. This interest transformed into a lifelong pursuit as he immersed himself in yoga and meditation during his teenage years, further augmenting his spiritual development with the conscientious use of psychedelics.

Working in the dynamic tech industry since the '90s, Orion has always nurtured a deep connection with his spiritual self, striking a harmonious balance between his professional life and metaphysical explorations. His journey took him from the sunny climes of Southern California to the vibrant San Francisco Bay Area and finally to the serene expanses of Nevada, each locale offering him unique perspectives that he continues to incorporate into his life.

Orion's personal journey has shaped the narrative of his book, reflecting the wisdom gleaned from countless books on metaphysics, philosophy, and self-growth, coupled with his experiential insights. His writing is a testament to his ability to traverse challenging mental and emotional landscapes and emerge with life skills that enrich both his personal and professional life.

Away from the keyboard and the tech world, Orion is a creator at heart. Music - particularly the transformative power of Electronic Dance Music, with Trance being a favorite - is his second language. He indulges this passion through both appreciation and creation, viewing it as another dimension of his expansive spiritual journey. His love for travel, exposure to different cultures, and quality time with his wife, their pets, and their now-grown children enrich his life and inspire his work.

Through this book, Orion aspires to spark 'a-ha' moments in his readers, guiding them to unearth the truths that already exist within them. His aim is not just to enlighten, but also to remind people of their intrinsic wisdom, contributing, in his way, to a more enlightened world. Journey with Orion Myst - remember, explore, and transform.

www.ingramcontent.com/pod-product-compliance
Lightning Source LLC
LaVergne TN
LVHW010611110826
845149LV00003B/864

* 9 7 9 8 9 8 8 6 5 0 3 3 1 *